This explanation text is best read from beginning to end, although the group could choose to take another look at various sections once they have finished reading through the book. If possible, give them a practical demonstration of the way a magnet works.

Contents

The front cover

What is the title of this book?

Can you see a magnet?

What is the boy doing with the magnet?

The back cover

What does the blurb tell us?

What do you think 'fascinating' means?

Contents

Which page tells us how to make a magnet?

What two things are on page 16?

What will be in the glossary?

READ

Read pages 2 and 3

Purpose: to understand why people use magnets,

to use the glossary.

EXPLORE

Pause at page 3

What are the people in the photographs doing?

What are they using the magnets for?

Why do you think the word 'metal' is in bold print?
(*It's in the glossary.* Help the children find it, if necessary,
by referring to the contents page.)

Look at the glossary and read what it says about 'metal'.

What do magnets do?

Magnets can help us do things.

Magnets:

- pick up pins,

- find **metal** in the sand,

- hold notes to the fridge,

- can be used to play games.

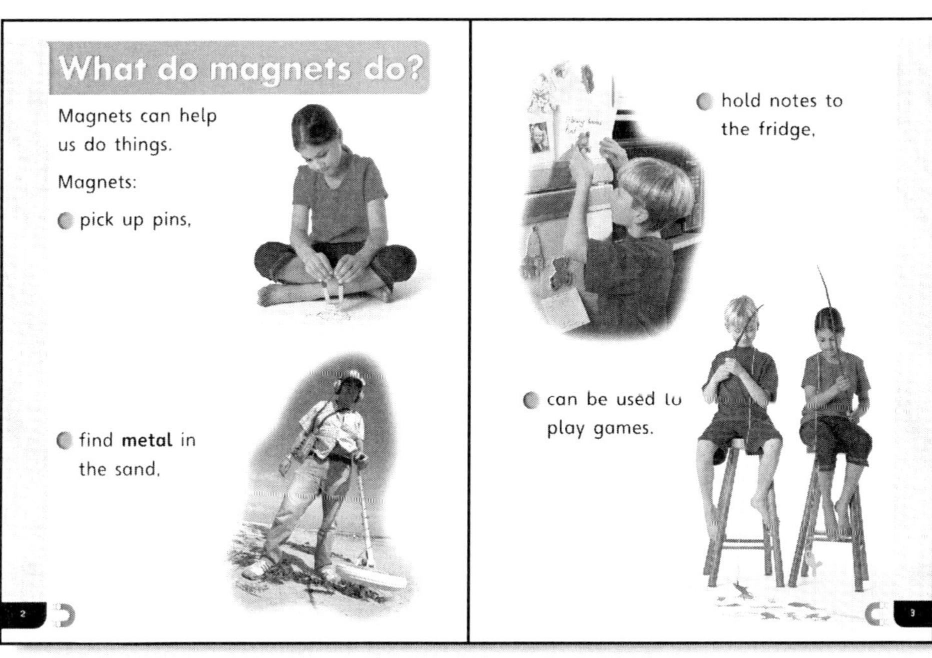

Read pages 4 and 5

Purpose: to find out if size is important in a magnet.

Pause at page 5

What is the heading on this spread?

Are the magnets on page 4 and page 5 the same size?

Which do you think is the stronger magnet?

Read pages 6 and 7

Purpose: to use the glossary,

to find out how a magnet works.

Pause at page 7

What three words on page 6 will be in the glossary?

Ask individual children to read the words and use the glossary to help them to understand what they mean.

Find the word 'magnetite' in the fact box. What smaller word can you find within it? (*magnet*)

What things cling to the magnet and what things will not be pulled to it?

What does an object need to have in it for the magnet to work? (*iron*)

What are magnets?

Magnets are metals that can pull some things towards them. They can also push some things away.

Metals with **iron** in them are pulled towards a magnet. Objects that **cling** to a magnet are **magnetic**.

All these things are magnetic because they have iron in them.

Objects made of plastic, wood or rubber are not magnetic. They won't be pulled to a magnet.

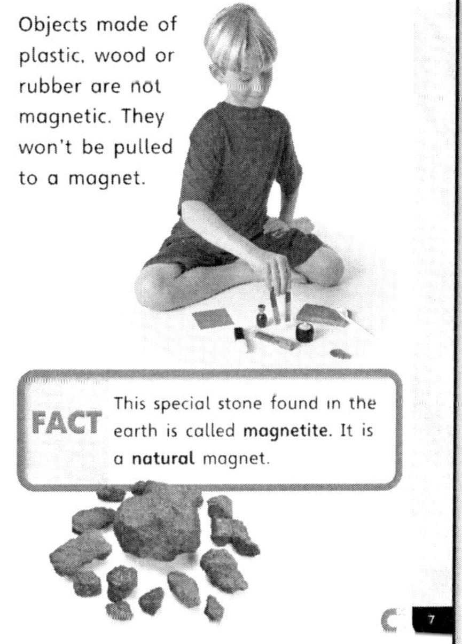

READ

Read pages 8 and 9

Purpose: to practise using the glossary,

to understand how the iron filings form
a pattern.

EXPLORE

Pause at page 9

Which words are in the glossary?

Look up the word 'force'.

Why will the iron filings be attracted to the magnet?

Read on your own and find out what makes the iron
filings form a pattern.

Magnetic force

Magnets are able to pull or push things because they have a special **force**. This force is called a magnetic force.

Watch what happens to these **iron filings**.

1. Put a piece of paper over a magnet.

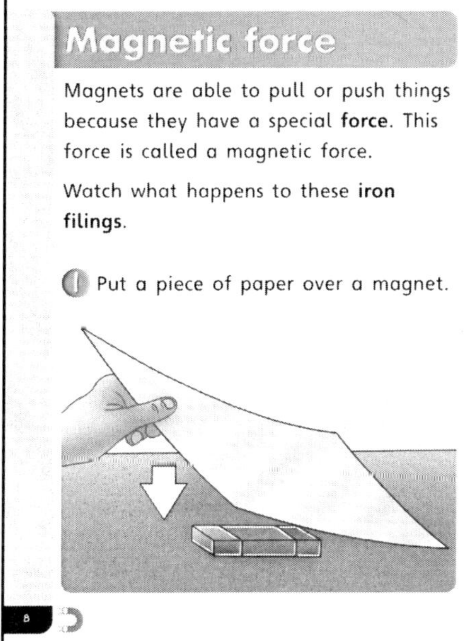

2. Sprinkle the iron filings on the paper. Give the paper a soft tap.

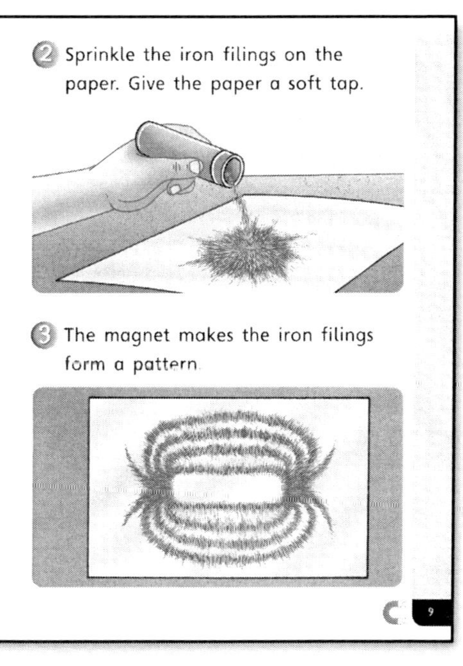

3. The magnet makes the iron filings form a pattern.

READ

Read pages 10 and 11

Purpose: to find out how to make a paper-clip magnet.

EXPLORE

Pause at page 11

What can you make on these pages?

Why do you think there are numbers on page 10? (*to show the order of the instructions*)

Read the text and find out what happens when you take the magnet away from the paper clips.

Make a magnet

When some metals touch a magnet, they become magnetic, too.

1. Put a paper clip on a magnet.

2. Add another paper clip to the first paper clip.

What happens?

3. Each paper clip becomes a magnet.

If you take the magnet away, the paper clips will stop being magnets.

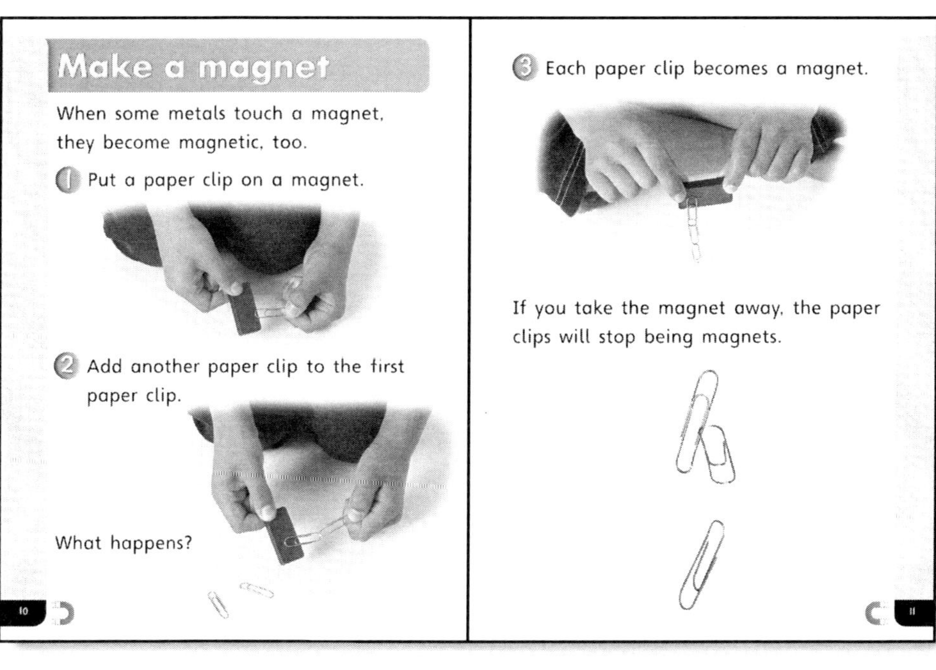

9

READ

Read pages 12 and 13

Purpose: to guess which things are magnetic, using what the children have learnt from the book.

EXPLORE

Pause at page 13

Read the title and the labels. (Play the guessing game with the group.)

What does an object have to have in it before it will be pulled towards a magnet? (*iron*)

(Praise the children who identified the objects correctly and who made good guesses.)

Tricky words (page 12):
Help the children with the word 'guessing' if they struggle.

Help the children with the silent 't' in 'whistle' if they struggle.

Magnet guessing game

Look at these things. Which do you think will be pulled towards a magnet?

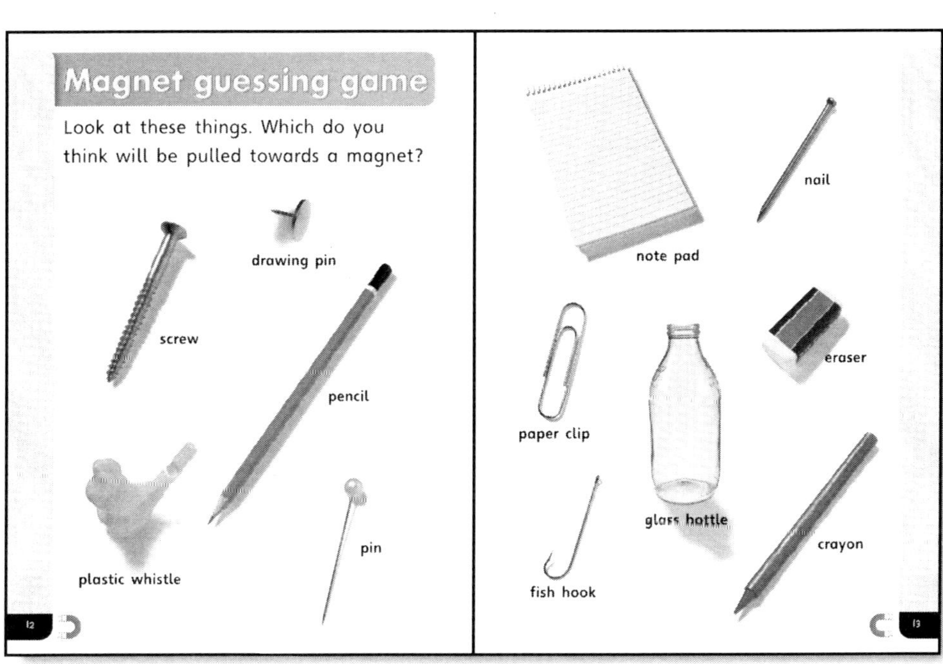

Read pages 14 and 15

Purpose: to confirm which things are magnetic and which are not.

Pause at page 14

What do all magnetic objects have in common?

Could the objects on this page become magnetic if they were put onto a magnet? (Make sure the children are clear that things without iron in them cannot be magnetic.)

Read page 15 on your own and find out if any of the objects have iron in them.

Magnetic

screw

nail

pin

drawing pin

fish hook

paper clip

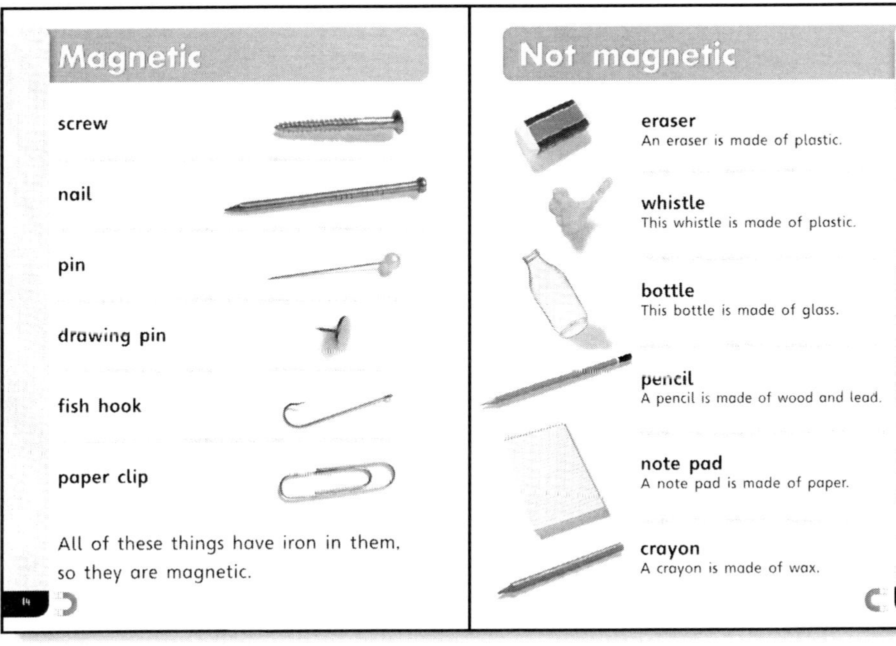

All of these things have iron in them,
so they are magnetic.

Not magnetic

eraser
An eraser is made of plastic.

whistle
This whistle is made of plastic.

bottle
This bottle is made of glass.

pencil
A pencil is made of wood and lead.

note pad
A note pad is made of paper.

crayon
A crayon is made of wax.

Read page 16

READ

Purpose: to recognise the features of a glossary.

Glossary

cling	to pull in and hold
force	anything that can cause a push or a pull
iron	a metal
iron filings	tiny pieces of iron
magnetic	able to be made into a magnet
magnetite	a stone that is magnetic
metal	strong, shiny material such as iron and steel
natural	found in or made by nature

Index

bottle 13, 15
crayon, 13, 15
drawing pin 6, 12, 14
eraser 13, 15
fish hook 13, 14
glass 13, 15
iron 6, 14
iron filings 8, 9
magnetic force 8
magnetite 7
metal 2, 4, 10
nail 6, 13, 14

note pad 13, 15
paper 8, 15
paper clip 6, 10, 11, 13, 14
pencil 12, 15
pin 6, 12, 14
plastic 7, 12, 13, 15
rubber 7
screw 12, 14
wax 15
whistle 12, 15
wood 7, 15

16

Pause at page 16

EXPLORE

What do you notice about the words in the glossary (*alphabetical order*)

What is a force?

What is magnetite?

Look at the index. How many pages mention paper clips?

(Ask someone to choose a word from the index and look up the relevant pages.)

After Reading
Revisit and Respond

- Start with a brief discussion of the features of *Magnets* that suggest it is a non-fiction book (*contains facts, no characters, need not be read in sequence, you can choose the pages you want to read*)

- What objects can you remember that a magnet attracts? (If possible have a magnet and the objects suggested on pages 12–13 for the children to try.)

- Why is a glossary useful? How do you know which words will be in the glossary? (*bold type*)

- Look at page 16. Can you find examples of a heading, a comma, alphabetical order?

- Look at the words in the glossary. Which words have you learnt about that you did not know before? (Encourage the children to memorise a word from the text – perhaps 'magnetic' – and write it down.)

Follow-up

Independent Group Activity Work

This book is accompanied by two photocopy masters, one with a reading focus, and one with a writing focus, which support the teaching objectives of this book. The photocopy masters can be found in the Planning and Assessment Guide.

PCM NF1.1 *(reading)*

PCM NF1.2 *(writing)*

You may also like to invite the children to read the text again during their independent reading (either at school or at home).

Writing

Guided writing: Discuss with the group the facts they have learned about magnets. Help them to present this information in a fact box with bullet points.

Extended writing: Choose a selection of magnetic and non-magnetic objects. Ask the children to list the things that are magnetic or not magnetic using pages 14–15 as a model.

Assessment Points

Assess that the children have learnt the main teaching focus of the book by checking that they can:

- explain organisational features of texts, including alphabetical order, layout, diagrams and captions.